Jack the Rascal

A biography of a very special Parson Jack Russell Terrier

John Plimmer

To Joanne without whose persuasion
I would never have known my lifelong
companion

Introduction

Dog lovers throughout the world will know exactly what I mean when I describe my own best friend as being unconditionally loyal and committed, without fear or favour. Having had the privilege of keeping such dedicated companions for most of my life, including a Staffordshire Bull Terrier, Poodle, Yorkshire Terrier and a dog of many breeds, one particular small yapper won over my heart from the first time I ever laid eyes on him as a two week old puppy. And now, as a sixteen year old veteran, he still remains my closest and unbiased ally; a Parson Jack Russell by the name of, strangely enough; Jack.

The reason for writing this biography of the most unusual canine I have ever known is because he is just that; unusual. His natural senses, understanding and analytical aptitude have always been of an exceptionally high standard, and on occasions, have left the onlooker in almost disbelief. In fact, our Jack is the closest four legged animal I have ever known to being human, without of course, the kind of partisan, bias beliefs, or emotional weaknesses that are contained within the human character.

My initial response to suggestions that I should write a book about 'Jack the Rascal' was one of obstinate rejection, on the grounds that there would not be sufficient material to fill the pages. But then, following a barrage of positives fired at me from various quarters, in particular from people who have known, Jack for many years, I have finally succumbed.

Once the decision was made, the historical research undertaken, mostly from my own memory, surprisingly reminded me that in fact, most of his life with us has been filled with adventurous, and at times, mischievous episodes, many of which strangers would have found it difficult to accept.

For a tail-wagger who has throughout his years, leapt from one crisis to another, it could be deemed fortuitous that this strong character survived so many perils, some of which were self-inflicted. There were many possibilities that we would lose him during his first year with us, including a widespread viral infection which affected most of the breed. After successfully fighting for his life and surviving such a perilous episode, I should have realised then, our four legged member of the family was indeed, a tough little feller, who possessed the kind of strong willed character rarely found in the majority of canines.

Such single-minded grit and resolve have remained with him since the day he was born, on 4 June 2001.

Jack has lived with us in the heart of the Meriden countryside, in the West Midlands, throughout his life, often taking on the role of a sheepdog, cattle rustler, wild cat stalker and rat exterminator. I am confident that if he had any idea that a book was being written about his exploits, my dog would take the bottom of my trouser leg, as he does every night when it's time to go to bed, and pull me away from the computer. He also has a canny knack of removing the duvet off me each morning, amazingly having never damaged it.

I shall be eternally grateful to Jack's Breeder, a charming and dedicated lady by the name of, Sara Nixon, who resides in Oxfordshire, for having provided me with a dog who has given us all, over sixteen years, a tremendous amount of pleasure.

Any one of the many exploits recorded in this book, might have applied to most breeds of dog, but it remains doubtful that all of them could have been attributed to just one.

Chapter One

The new member of the family

It was on a bright, sunny spring morning back in 2001, as we walked briskly across the open fields, admiring the new born lambs that were prancing about around their mothers. My daughter, Jo asked, "When is the new puppy due, Dad?" At the time we were crossing over a narrow wooden bridge, built over a small stream dividing one large field from another, and which from its ancient, and weathered appearance, might well have been constructed in the time of, Queen Victoria, having not seen a lick of paint since.

There were two Mallards resting nearby at the waters edge, a Drake and his Hen companion, which both turned their heads our way, as if impatient to hear the answer I was about to give. Until that time, I had participated in long walks on a daily basis, trying to introduce some physical balance into my life, having spent perhaps more hours than is deemed healthy, sitting at a computer writing novels.

"I should say in a couple of weeks yet, Jo," I answered, knowing the due date for our new addition to the family was in fact, the fourth of June.

It had been Jo's initial idea to get a dog, finally persuading me that such a companion would benefit greatly from all the walking I constantly undertook. It would also mean I would have some other subject to concentrate on, in addition to my story writing. Who could argue with such a logical and commonsensical suggestion, especially as I had been a dog lover for most of my life?

Having had the privilege of living with a Parson Jack Russell Terrier many years before, as a schoolboy, I had always had a deep rooted leaning towards the breed. I was aware they were extremely loyal, if not mischievous and fearless. Each had their own individual lovable character, so it had been decided the newcomer to the family would be one of those cheeky faced, rat exterminators.

Having contacted the Kennel Club in London, who recommended Sara Nixon, a Parson Jack Russell breeder in Oxford, I had confirmed with the lady that a litter was close to being born. Since making that call, most of the conversation that took place at home had been focused on the new comer to the family.

I must admit to having felt a little excitement at the prospect of being constantly reminded of my youth, having spent a great deal of that particular period in the company of the same lineage of dog named Russ; a Jack Russell Terrier who had been extremely devoted all those years earlier. Memories of adventurous close encounters, chases and confrontations came flooding back, and much of the subject matter of this book, could quite easily have been attributed to Russ.

"Is he likely to tear up the furniture?"

"What if he becomes ill?"

"Who's going to feed him?"

"What are we going to call him?"

The questions did the rounds, to which we always had a logical and satisfactory answer.

Now, it goes without saying, if you call your first Jack Russell, 'Russ' then that doesn't exactly show a great deal of innovation in deciding his name. Thus, it was the same with the new dog.

"He will be named Jack," I insisted one day, "After the name of his breed."

No one seemed to argue about that, although I supposed I could have been just a little more adventurous, such as selecting a name like, Hades, after the Greek God, or perhaps, Lubet, after the nineteenth century French President. But no; Jack it was to be.

"What if he's a girl?"

"He will be a dog," I again insisted, not that I had anything against bitches; it was just that all of my previous dogs had been of that same sex.

The breeder, Sara Nixon, had invited us down to Oxford to view the litter when it would be two weeks old, at the same time confirming we would not be allowed to take our selected puppy home with us until it was at least six weeks old, and had been subjected to its initial vaccinations, which again was logical and acceptable. And yet, unknown to the rest of my family, I found myself actually counting the days.

Finally, the time arrived for us to travel down to the University City to see the litter of puppies for the first time. We were made extremely welcome and escorted into the back kitchen of the house, where the puppies were scampering about, watched over by their mother. There were two dogs included in the boisterous group, one of which had already been sold, leaving just a mournful looking soul with a pure white body, and black and tan markings on his face. He had distinguishing white mottling on his left ear and the largest pair of brown sorrowful eyes I had ever seen in a dog, as if feeling abandoned, having not yet been adopted at just two weeks.

"Why are you looking so sad little man?" I commented, as I picked up this scrupulously clean little feller for the very first time, who was not much bigger than the palm of my outstretched hand.

"Don't be fooled by his expression," Sara pointed out, "He's the strongest of the litter, and always the first to get to his mother's milk."

In fact, we stayed long enough to watch the hustle and bustle at feeding time, and quickly realised that, Sara had not exaggerated. Our puppy fought robustly to be the first in the queue for the nourishment each of his brother and sisters were craving for.

Following that exercise, my daughter sat with newly born Jack on her lap, her eyes filled with love and adoration, whilst I confirmed various issues with Sara, including his Kennel Club name, which was to be 'Gone to Ground Meriden Jack'; although to us he would always be known as just plain and simple, Jack.

Before we left on that first introductory visit, I spent some time just sitting back and watching our new puppy from a distance, admiring what appeared to be a self-reliant nature displayed by his various mannerisms. He certainly appeared to stand out from the crowd, but that impression might well have been the partisan result of him having been chosen by us. He was inquisitive, and must have been wondering what on earth these two legged creatures were doing there, giving him all of their attention. But, I was aware that we had a long way to go before the bonding process between dog and humans would be completed successfully, although I did strangely feel I was already close to this particular young jasper.

I was also aware that, this impressive little dog, would undoubtedly be taking over our lives, but at that time, had no idea how much real joy and happiness he would be bestowing upon us all, during the many years which were to follow. There is an old saying that you should never wish away your life, yet after we left, and on the drive back home from Oxford, the count-down had already begun, and neither myself nor my daughter could wait for the following four weeks to pass by.

When we arrived home, it was all about Jack the Terrier, with Jo delivering a vivid description of the future new family member to her mother, who I should confirm, had some reservations about enlarging the nest with the introduction of a canine. But in a kind of mild, insidious way, we both knew that once my wife, Ann, had laid eyes on the bundle of fun coming her way, any doubts would quickly disappear.

Sara Nixon could not have been more helpful, advising us with regard to food and bedding; even games our new puppy would love to play, and when we returned on that day of celebration to finally collect and take Jack home, we were well prepared. It was certainly a day to remember, and the first thing I noticed was how, Jack had grown twice his size during that interim period.

I was given a list of responsibilities to be fulfilled, including a need to keep the puppy indoors until he had received his second inoculations at our own local vets. We were also advised to give the dog lots of time to settle into his new surroundings, and if possible, allow him eventually, to socialise with other puppies, which as time predicted, was easier said than done.

Sat wrapped up in a blanket on my daughter's lap, our new puppy viewed us with those same large brown eyes, looking perplexed, as we drove up the motorway towards home. Two very excited beings, with me finding it difficult to sustain an adult approach to the new venture.

When we arrived home, our suspicions about my wife's attitude towards the puppy, proved to be well founded, and she could hardly put the newcomer down, after being introduced.

Jack's biggest treat was still a couple of weeks away, when following his second inoculations, he would be introduced to a vast landscape of green fields, streams, wild life and trees upon which he could practice raising his leg when relieving himself. I couldn't wait to have his shiny snow-like coat accompany me on my daily walks, although we all followed Sara's instructions to the letter.

During those first couple of weeks, our new friend was confined to the back garden, and his energy was spent chasing a broom head, which we all took turns in swinging around. Alas, at a time when we believed all was going well, Jack was unexpectedly subjected to a minor disaster, which had quite a traumatic effect on me also.

We had placed his blanketed bed in the laundry room, from which the back door could be accessed. A pane of heavily patterned glass was set inside the door panel, with a small window at the side, allowing sufficient light to penetrate into the small room. I knew he would have to be given time to settle into his new surroundings, and thought it wise to begin as we meant to continue, by closing the door separating the laundry room with the rest of the house, once I had put Jack to bed each night.

He had only been with us for a matter of days, before one particular dark night brought quite a severe thunderstorm. The night sky rumbled and echoed with loud crashes and vibrating thunder, accompanied by impressive flashes of lightening, which lit up the surrounding countryside. It was most certainly the kind of traumatic drama that would have sent the most committed fur and feather night stalkers, fleeing for the cover of their nests and dens. Unfortunately, it also had the same effect on, Jack, who was confined to the laundry room.

Oblivious to any sound coming from the puppy's restricted domicile, I assumed he was sleeping through the noise of the storm. It wasn't until later I realised just how wrong my assumption had been.

When I went downstairs early the following morning, I found the dog still trembling in fear. His eyes told me the story of a night of terror for such a young feller, and on the door jam I could see scarring where the petrified puppy had tried to gnaw his way through the wood.

The waves of guilt that swept over me were almost unbearable, and from that very minute, his bed was moved into the larger and more spacious kitchen area. He was never to be so confined at night, ever again.

Once he had made his first visit to the vets for a check up, and had successfully received his second inoculations, it was finally the time to let him find his feet in the open fields. As soon as we led him through the back gate and undid his lead, that was it. He ran, and ran, and ran, stopping only occasionally to view a flock of grazing sheep, or gaze in wonderment at a small herd of cattle occupying a corner of a field. Everything that was new to him; every small bridge; gatepost; woolly sheep, stream and wooden fence, was inquisitively scrutinised. Soon, he would become accustomed to every crook and cranny of the many open fields we would happily stride across. This was to be his new life, and he never fell short of showing his pleasure in his new playground, and panoramic landscape surroundings.

He was an instant success with other members of our small community, wagging his tail and standing up on his hind legs, whenever anyone stopped on the street to stroke and make a fuss of him. I must admit to enjoying a great deal of pride from knowing that I was the owner of such an attractive looking dog, one that others could not avoid laying their hands on.

At that time I was commissioned by the House of Stratus, a London based publishers, to write a series of novels, and would spend many hours each day alone in the house, with both my daughter and wife at work. Our son, Neil was also away in the Royal Navy, so the solitude helped a great deal when working in my study, with Jack sitting on top of my desk.

He would spend hours watching me work, like a young apprentice trying to figure out what the purpose was of playing a keyboard like a piano. The majority of his day would be spent up on that desk top, either sleeping or observing. And when he thought it was time for me to take a break, he would tug at my sleeve, which was the signal given for a repeat visit to the outback and beyond. This lad had more guile, antics and tricks up his sleeve at such an early age, than most humans.

Very soon we worked out a pattern of play for each day, and a schedule was introduced, which we both abided by. I would work on a couple of draft chapters, while Jack watched. Then the sleeve would be tugged and we would disappear from the house for an hour or so. Having returned to the computer, he would then have a nap, and so on and so forth. It was a roster that lasted for a few years to come, interrupted only when someone rang the bell on the front door. You could easily imagine what took place when that occurred.

Without actually realising what was taking place, our daily habits were slowly evolving towards a one man, one dog relationship. Where ever I went, so did Jack.

Chapter Two

Lost and Found

We all felt it was important to afford, Jack a marked out space which would be his territory, one which he could claim was his alone, and from which we thought would give him some independence, and perhaps help in developing his confidence, not that he required much more. So, the little feller was allotted his own soft chair in the lounge, protected by a heavy blanket, and which he was immediately encouraged to use. He wasted little time in recognising that this was to be his retreat, when not using his bed in the kitchen.

From the chair he would lie down and observe the rest of the room, and it quickly became apparent that miming my own characteristics, was yet another talent he was developing. For instance, I would sit in my chair with the dog's eyes transfixed on my every move. If I stretched, so would Jack. When I deliberately yawned, so did Jack. At first, I was doubtful whether I was assessing his behaviour correctly, and progressed to stretching one arm upright above my head.

For a time, he just looked and observed, obviously confused as to how he could replicate the movement. Eventually, he just rolled over on to his back with one leg stretched vertically in the air. Such a presentation was amazing, and from there on, he slept in that position with legs apart and failing to conceal all that he owned. But above all, I instantly recognised that this was one hell of an intelligent dog.

Jack continued his miming acts when out on the field, watching new born lambs prancing with four straight legs bouncing off the ground. Very quickly he somehow learned to do the same, and I shall never forget the sight of a Jack Russell Terrier, prancing about as if he was one of the lambs.

As the months rolled by, more surprising antics and aspects of his character came to the fore, resulting in a great deal of amusement for those of us who witnessed his various unexpected presentations. Barking when the sound from the television was too loud; sitting upright before me, when he knew to the exact minute, the time for his final night time walk. In fact, his inner clock took him beyond that. At the exact time I would usually retire to bed, he would pull at my trouser leg. He even knew when the window cleaner was due, and would sit in the downstairs front window watching and waiting, for about five minutes before the lad arrived with his ladder. And all of this was going on during the first six months he was with us.

There is a belief in some dog breeding quarters that you can never lose a Jack Russell Terrier, and although I would never dream of putting such a claim to the test, unfortunately on one occasion, Jack did.

Lozells is an inner-city district of Birmingham; an industrious and extremely busy part of the second largest city in the country, and situated about nine miles from where we live. It was during Jack's first autumn with us, that we were compelled to visit Lozells to collect some business supplies. The sky was cloaked with black clouds, from which heavy rain cascaded down throughout that day and for most of the following night. People hurried about their daily business beneath umbrellas, or with their heads bowed down before the windswept rain, concentrating solely on avoiding the puddles.

Jack by then had become accustomed to travelling in the car, and would occupy the back seat. If we had to leave him, we made sure it wasn't for long, and on this occasion, after parking the car, we checked to ensure one of the windows was slightly open for his benefit, and to allow air to circulate inside the vehicle. We knew that we would only be absent for a few minutes, so were not concerned about leaving him. Neither were any of us aware that our worst nightmare was about to become a reality.

Even now, neither myself, my wife or daughter, have any idea how it happened on that terrible and depressing day, but having been away from the vehicle for no more than ten minutes, when we returned, the dog had disappeared.

The car's doors remained locked, and the open window was, as I had left it, no more than one inch down from the closed position. But what we faced was the undisputed fact that the vehicle was empty, and Jack was missing.

My initial thought was that someone had taken him, but there again, all the doors remained locked when we returned to the car. I even looked in the boot to confirm that was empty, which it surely was. The whole affair was a complete mystery, and without wasting any further time, we began a conscientious search of the surrounding busy streets, calling his name out aloud, and asking if anyone had seen a Jack Russell Terrier, but no one had, obviously too busy in making their way through the heavy rain. We must have spent hours exercising our legs and looking in every conceivable nook and cranny, where it might have been likely for a small dog to hide or become trapped, and continuing to scour through the immediate vicinity surrounding our parked car, but without success. Finally, we had to accept it was hopeless. By some mysterious method or design, we had lost our much beloved Jack.

It was difficult to think objectively, and feeling enormously distressed by the loss of our four legged companion, we managed to visit a local police station to report him missing. A detailed description was given to the desk sergeant, who did his best to reassure us that there was a good possibility that our dog would eventually turn up. In those days, the police actually made a record of a missing dog, which would be checked against any strays found and taken into police custody. I was advised to keep ringing the station to see if any dog similar to Jack's description, had been taken in.

There was only one official dogs home, which existed in the whole of the city centre in those days, and which had the legend, The Home for Lost and Starving Dogs, across its doors. As a last resort, we visited the establishment and asked the staff there if they would make a note of our Jack's description, just in case he was found and taken directly to them. They obliged us, but I knew that in reality, there was little hope of that happening.

It was dark by the time I revisited Lozells, and for a second time, searched the streets near to where we had parked up earlier, still trying hard to identify the manner in which he could have possibly escaped from the vehicle, but to no avail.

The Lozells Police must have been getting fed up with this bloke constantly pestering them, enquiring whether any dog similar to Jack in appearance had been taken in there. Eventually, I ran out of ideas and submitted to complete surrender. I was void of any other ideas, or ways in which we could continue to track him down. All of our endeavours to find him had been exhausted. All the planes were up, as they used to say in the war films, and there was nothing more we could have done.

It was in a solemn mood and distraught manner in which we eventually returned home, having given up all hope of ever seeing our little friend again. My last enquiry with the police was at eleven o'clock that night, with the same result as I had experienced previously.

I remember standing alone and looking down at his empty bed, with an overwhelming feeling of guilt and despondency. It was dark, wet and cold outside, and my dog was somewhere out there, lost and vulnerable to, God only knew what.

Finally I retired to bed, but found sleep hard to come by. My mind was in turmoil and the last thing I wanted was to snatch a piece of unconsciousness that would temporarily remove me from the same world in which I feared my dog was suffering. Never before had I fretted so much about a four legged animal. In my disquiet, I must have eventually dozed off, because at about three o'clock in the morning, I suddenly awoke with a start. I had no idea what had brought me so abruptly out of my unsettled slumber and for a moment, sat up in bed, staring through the darkness and listening to any unusual night sound; but there was none.

I reached a point at which I was accepting that in all probability, I must have been dreaming, and whatever had been playing on my mind, had caused me to stir so abruptly. Then, as I was about to lie down once again, a sound reached my ears. Barely audible; there was a slight noise coming from downstairs. At first I wondered if it was the sound of the rain lashing against the front door, but quickly dismissed that notion, when I heard it again. It was definitely confirmation of something scratching on the front door. Could it be that Jack had found his way home? No; again that was too preposterous to even contemplate.

As I hurried down the stairs in my pyjamas, I still remained unsure as to whether I had dreamt the sounds I thought I had heard. Not bothering to turn any lights on, I quickly opened the door, and was shocked to see the figure of a totally exhausted and soaking wet, Jack Russell Terrier lying there on the paving outside.

It took all of his remaining strength for, Jack to look up at me with such a pitiful sorrowful expression in his eyes. In similar fashion to a long distance runner that had overstepped his mark, he lay on his stomach, gasping for breath. For a moment I stood there frozen to the spot, unable to accept the reality of the scene that lay at my bare feet.

I collected his small limp body from off the ground and held him close to me in both arms, before taking my fragile friend into the kitchen and placing him carefully on top of a towel. I was so overjoyed, I was actually shaking with excitement and couldn't utter a word. Was I actually still asleep and dreaming all of this?

Quickly, I got to work, toweling him down, as he could barely stand with his eyes closed. Jack was falling to sleep as I continued to rub him down. Having made sure he was completely dry and warm, it was obvious he needed lots of sleep and rest, but not before I got some food and drink into him. Once satisfied he would recuperate, I knelt down beside him and watched as he closed his eyes once again, and wondered off into a well deserved bout of slumber.

That dog, who at the time was only a few months old, had actually found his way home from some nine miles away, and having to somehow deal with all kinds of obstacles that would have been thrown his way. A multitude of streets occupied by heavy traffic, side streets and motorways would have had to have been confronted, before finally arriving back in Meriden. How on earth had he managed to circumvent Spaghetti Junction, which would have been a major and dangerous obstruction? What he had achieved was as nigh on impossible, as the fact, he had escaped from the car in the first place.

At that moment, I could only believe some kind of miracle had taken place, but there again remembered those words declaring that a Jack Russell Terrier could never be lost.

I spent most of the remainder of that night at Jack's side, listening to his breathing, as he dreamt away the hours, until finally satisfied that there was nothing more to be done, and confident that he would now recover from what must have been an extremely challenging and traumatic ordeal for one so young, I at last, retired to my own bed.

The following morning, I was awakened by my lost and found companion jumping on to the bed, and letting me know it was time for his walk. Had it been a miracle that had taken place during that previous day and night? I had no idea. I was just thankful we had got him back. Now, when I recall the incident, still unaware of how he got out of that vehicle, whilst parked in one of the city's busiest districts, I am convinced that his way home was a result of pure instinct, and the perseverance and tracking ability of the breed of dog to which Jack belongs.

The fact that a Jack Russell can never be lost is absolutely true and I bear witness to that phenomenon. Following that incident, even when he accompanied me on many long journeys, Jack was never again, left alone in any vehicle.

Chapter Three

The Rat Catcher

In recent years, the dramatic increase in the rodent population has customarily brought about a greater demand for the services of official rat catchers, employed by various councils throughout the country. Whether infestations have been discovered in urban or rural areas, the controllers of vermin have been kept extremely busy, resulting in some quarters, fear that the constant uses of substances supplied by the official exterminators, have been losing their effect on the rat population. Vermin have gradually become immune to the life threatening entities offered.

Of course, it is widely accepted that Jack Russell Terriers are effective rat catchers, and from my own personal experience I can vouch for such a belief being true. It's in the dogs genes; their pedigree and breeding. In locations where these small energetic dogs are active, rodents are virtually non existent.

It has been well evidenced and leaves little doubt that these terriers possess by nature, a primary instinct to kill wild vermin that bring with them disease and danger to humans. The Jack Russell does not require any special training, when it comes to ridding buildings and open spaces of infestations. Their success in diminishing the rat population comes from a natural ability, and our Jack was no exception. Coupled with a constant desire to play, and persistently tease anything on four legs that was slower than the speed of movement he had been blessed with, he became well rehearsed in testing his abilities with grazing sheep.

As with most dogs of that breed, once he discovered his four legs could carry him at high speeds across any kind of terrain, his favourite occupation was to pester Ewes, knowing there was no possibility of being caught. It was a past time however, that was forbidden during the time the sheep were carrying lambs, obviously to avoid subjecting them to any level of anxiety, which could be dangerous to both them and the lambs they would be carrying.

As the farm woollies would be peaceably grazing in the early morning sunshine, a white object would frequently be seen stealthily crawling towards some unaware Ewe. In similar fashion to a fox stalking its prey, he would slowly drag his stomach along the ground in utter silence and anticipation, until he reached a point where his target would eventually spot the would-be intruder. Inevitably the Ewe would straighten up and stamp her two hoofs purposefully, in an effort to make known her objections and frighten the interloper away.

Jack would respond accordingly, by standing up on all four legs, before staring his adversary out, and challenging her to force him to move.

When the sheep had gathered sufficient nerve to move even closer to her opponent, showing no fear, but plenty of annoyance, he would remain motionless, until she was within striking distance. Then, as far as he was concerned, the most playful part of the game would be introduced by turning and swiftly running away, with the Ewe not having the slightest chance of catching him.

With his tail frantically wagging, he would then return and repeat the same playful motions, until I decided to call it a day, and would order him to stop. It was Jack's favourite game, which perhaps tumbled into the realms of farcical badinage, when he would play out the ultimate role of behaving in a similar fashion to a sheep dog.

On a number of occasions, when we were out walking, my attention would be diverted elsewhere, such as meeting a friend and stopping to chat, or when I became engrossed in watching a Hawk gliding on the wing in search of prey, my four legged friend would take advantage and make his unilateral move. The field full of sheep would suddenly become vacant, only for me to find them all huddled together in one corner, with Jack holding them in a tight group by running to and fro, mimicking the farmer's highly trained sheep minders. And yet, the woollies never seemed to become over bothered by this pretender, and for most of the time they would continue with their grazing, after being driven to whichever part of the field, Jack preferred them to occupy.

It was all good fun, as long as I kept a check on my companion, and no harm came from his playful antics, which was never the case.

On one occasion, as I stood with, Richard the farmer, both of us chuckling at my dog's tomfoolery, my friend quipped, "Well now, if ever I need a replacement dog, that lad of yours would fit the bill."

"You just let me know, Richard, if you ever need any additional help in moving the sheep," I jokingly answered.

Of course, like most young terriers, he would chase anything with fur on its back, but never actually caught anything, although the opportunities to do so were frequent. It was the chase that appealed to him, rather than actually catching his prey and causing any injury.

One day, he found a small injured Blue Tit on the back garden lawn, and stood at its side sniffing and displaying the caring side of his character, by gently licking the bird. There was certainly no sign of any desire to harm the feathered casualty, and Jack's instinct told him the bird was in trouble. In fact, it was in desperate need of a safe haven in which it could spend some time recovering, having somehow damaged a wing.

After carefully placing our injured visitor on to a bed of cotton wool contained in an open cardboard box, I placed it on a high shelf in the garage to keep the bird safe from predators. It was then duly nursed over a period of two weeks, being fed daily on crushed and prepared meal, and milk, until the damaged wing repaired itself and the Blue Tit was strong enough to fly away, back to its natural habitat.

Throughout that period of constant care and monitoring, Jack would station himself outside the closed garage door, and each time I visited the injured Blue Tit, he would be there. After following me into the garage, he would then sit at my feet, waiting for an update on the casualty's progress.

"He's doing fine, Jack," I would tell him, before he would leave the garage to take up his post outside. Strangely, I was the only person in the household allowed entry into that garage during the time our injured visitor remained inside. Each time another member of the family attempted to enter, the four legged guard would create Merry Hell. As far as he was concerned, the feathered patient belonged to him and me, and that was an end to it.

There were only two living creatures to which Jack was a threat. For some unknown reason, he took an immense disliking from an early age, to Ravens and large black birds. Often, he would sprint off in chase of one that had just landed, and on one occasion, he actually killed a Raven, as it struggled to get off the ground in time.

Whether his hatred for this species of bird was a result of the way they used to caw as they landed, or because we had both seen them on several occasions, land on top of a lamb's head and peck out its eyes, resulting in eventual death, which was a curse to old Richard, and certainly distressing to ourselves.

The other furry animal Jack took an instant dislike to, was for different reasons. Throughout his life, rats always remained his priority target, and being a Jack Russell Terrier, it was his natural habit to kill them; a task he never shied away from whenever an opportunity arose.

Not so long ago, it was reported in one national newspaper that a Parson Jack Russell had gone missing from its place of work, which was a large factory complex somewhere up north. Apparently the dog was absent for approximately three weeks, before the workers noticed an unpleasant odour coming from the air ventilation system.

The Fire Brigade were called to the premises, and fire fighters managed to gain access into the system. Instead of finding the corpse of a small dog, which had fearfully been anticipated, they discovered banks of dead rats piled high, with a Parson Jack Russell greeting them with a wagging tail. The dog must have been dead on its feet, as the final count of his work totalled over three hundred rodents, all seen off by the little dog who had just been doing its job.

I am confident that Jack would have accomplished the same tally if given the chance. His ability to move and strike fast was enhanced by his acute hearing and sense of smell. On occasions I would wait until he was about fifty yards away from the house, at the gate which gave access to the fields. I would then stand inside the hallway, and quietly tinkle the keys to the front door. Amazingly, he would respond by racing back inside the house, having picked up the sound of the keys.

I repeated the same exercise on a number of occasions, only because I found it difficult to believe his hearing was so sensitive.

The open countryside at the back of where we live is separated from gardens by a Hawthorn hedge, which must have stood proud for many years before the houses were built. Not too far away, the gardens of a local hotel back on to the same hedgerow, and it was common knowledge the establishment had been plagued in the past by rats. There was no doubt that those particular unwanted rodents would work their way along the Hawthorn hedge seeking food, in particular any nuts contained within bird feeders introduced into the gardens.

In our own garden, we used to delight in watching many different birds visiting our own bird feeders. Tits of all denominations would be joined by Robins and other feathered species. I have been frequently delighted to observe pheasants suddenly appear in the garden, having come off the fields, before vacating it through the hedge row at the bottom. On one occasion, we had a Woodpecker come calling, and then a Hawk, which sat for some time devouring its lunch, obviously freshly caught in its claws.

With Wood Pigeons waiting patiently on the ground beneath the feeders, to snap up any tit-bits falling from where smaller birds were feeding, the whole area became industriously supported by nature herself. Squirrels would also put in the occasional appearance, working hard to gain access to the nuts, but usually without having much success, so we used to place a handful or so of nuts on the ground for both the squirrels and Wood Pigeons. And then there was the occasional rat, whose presence would scatter those already in occupation, not knowing it was dicing with instant death.

On occasions, particularly during the evenings, as the dusk was beginning to settle, Jack would suddenly be aroused from his chair, and race towards the closed back door, amazingly without making a peep, but looking for me to release him from the confines of the house.

Each time that happened, I knew exactly what was in his mind, and would instantly open the back door, and stand back, as the dog would fly across the garden towards the hedge row at the bottom. A distant squeal of surprise would then be heard, and yet another dead rat would be hurled over the gate into the field, before the dog would return to the house with a look of satisfaction in his eyes. Inevitably, the number of rats that visited our garden quickly diminished, until they vanished completely.

It all sounds very macabre, but such practices were natural to a Jack Russell Terrier, in the same way as animals in the wild, hunt each other for food in order to survive; only Jack never used to eat his prey.

On one occasion, a friend and neighbour once called to me, as he wanted to show me something he described as being, 'highly unusual'. I walked with him back to his house and through the open door of his garage, which led to his back garden.

"I think he's brought us a present," my friend claimed.

There, sitting in the middle of my neighbour's back lawn was my dog, with both ears pointed upwards, on full alert, with his tongue hanging out. In front of him, lying expired on the ground, was the biggest rat I had ever clapped eyes on. Of course, Jack was instructed to remove the vermin and take it to the fields, which he did with some reluctance. That incident was repeated again with other neighbours, who luckily took each instance jocularly and in good heart. It was obvious that the dog wanted to announce his success to others, and was never shy in putting himself in the limelight.

Unfortunately, as he reached old age, and his natural senses diminished, and his speed of movement dramatically slowed, the rats returned with a vengeance, and we had to get the local rat catcher to attend, and do the same job that our dog had been doing for years. Once again, a major infestation was removed, but without any assistance from the Jack Russell Terrier, who was by then in retirement.

Chapter Four

Sheep Shearing

One early spring, the sudden appearance of fourteen young bullocks in our field pleasantly surprised us all. The farmer made it quite clear he intended leaving the beasts there throughout the summer to graze off the land, in the hope they would be sufficiently fattened by the time autumn was upon us. They would then be sold to the highest bidder for either breeding or being sold on at market.

Their presence certainly added interest to our daily lives throughout that period, and we enthusiastically observed them moving from one grazing patch to another, approaching us whenever we appeared close by. They were always in an inquisitive, but friendly mood, and never presented any problems to ourselves or other passing hikers.

The only nervous individual within our small group was, Jack. Each time he accompanied me, the dog would always steer clear of the small group of Bovines, and in return, would only warrant a few glances, and certainly nothing more. Until, that is, one day we were both in the top field, and the bullocks were lying down basking in the sun, at the side of a stream in the bottom field, which was a fair distance away.

They all looked so peaceful and contented, and

my thoughts were disturbed by the realisation that, towards the end of the year, the majority, if not all, would be sold off and taken for slaughter. Since living where we were, and coming into contact with so many sheep and cattle on a daily basis, both lamb and beef were rare dishes in our house. We all found it difficult, and still do, in eating the same meat that was in fact, standing and grazing just a few yards away from where we live.

Anyway, when the time came to head for home, once again, Jack took the lead and crossed over the bridge into the field where the bullocks were dozing, leaving me a good hundred yards or so behind. I wasn't concerned because he knew his way home, and always waited for me to catch up in any case.

Why the dog suddenly decided to get closer to the other occupants of the field I will never really know, but I suspect his sudden burst of bravery came as a result of the bullocks lying down on the ground peacefully, without presenting any threat to him. Well, at least that was what I thought at the time.

As I drew nearer, I could see Jack following his upturned nose towards the young cattle, drawing closer and closer by the minute, with both ears pointed, which confirmed he was moving with the utmost alertness, until he was proudly standing amongst them. He cheekily stood there, in the very centre of the small group, motionless for some time, occasionally turning his head to look at each and every one of them.

In response, they did nothing and continued to lazily feel the heat of the sun on their backs. If I had been in possession of a camera at that moment, the resulting photograph would have been interesting.

It was all so serene, although I looked on with a little concern. Then, without warning, one of the bullocks suddenly got to his feet, causing Jack to freeze and remain standing his ground. He obviously had not been expecting such a surprised maneuver.

When the young bovine turned its head and stared directly at the small intruder, Jack stared back at him, having to lift his head to obtain eye level. But, unlike his antics with the sheep, this time his strategy failed, and realising he was about to be robustly removed from the group, lost his nerve and flew away from the group, heading up the field.

Well, at least he had the speed to stay clear of his adversary, until the bullock would get tired of the chase. If that's what Jack was thinking, he was soon to realise he had made a dreadful mistake.

I stood and continued to watch as the performance unfolded, in similar fashion to some Brian Rix farce.

As Jack took off, heading up the field towards home, the bullock chased after him, which I must admit was something I hadn't expected. The one thing about cattle was the fact they never over exercised unless it was absolutely necessary.

Anyway, I continued to watch, as Jack stopped and turned to face his pursuer, but the bullock continued heading towards the dog with its head bowed down, as if readying itself to charge. That in itself was also a surprise.

Jack took off again, but the bullock didn't even slow down. He kept chasing after the dog at an uninterrupted canter, obviously convinced that this impertinent canine required a lesson to be taught in manners.

I began to walk again, in the same direction the pair had taken, passing the other bullocks that were still lying down, unperturbed and without a care in the world. Again, I watched the display ongoing further up the field. My dog stopping in its tracks, turning to face the bullock, before being disappointed as the mass of muscle continued heading towards him.

Jack repeated his maneuver on a number of occasions, but it made no difference. He barked out aloud, but the larger animal was showing an unusual determination to catch the dog, and any attempt to scare it off just wasn't going to work.

So, finally, Jack turned for the last time and increased his running speed, heading towards our own back gate, with the same bullock also appearing to accelerate. It was still all too unbelievable, and I couldn't help but smile to myself.

I just about caught sight of my dog disappearing through the gate into our back garden, and became fearful that his stalker would do the same. Thankfully, the larger animal finally decided to give up the chase. It just stood there, staring over the hedgerow, obviously puzzled as to why the small whipper snapper was hiding in some place that wasn't a field.

By the time I arrived at the back gate, the bullock had moved away, and I found my courageous young companion, cowering at the back door. After that incident, each time we stepped into the same field occupied by the young bovines, Jack went on the lead, and was kept at a fairly good distance.

Although, barely a day did not go by without him being taken out on to the fields, another treat for him was to be taken each morning up into the village to get the daily newspapers. Next to the newsagents is a small library, where I used to tether him to a flower box outside the front, before leaving him to go and purchase copies of the daily news. When I returned, in most instances, someone would be at his side chatting away, and he would be sitting on the pavement, as if listening to every word.

There were those in fact, who carried various treats in their pockets, and who would stop to give him one, in return for him allowing them to stroke him. One particular elderly lady would appear without fail, and offer a small treat, which would be taken with enthusiasm. In return, Jack would always thank the lady by licking her hand. These people were true dog lovers who were caring and loving towards any canine, no matter what breed they were, but having seen, Jack grow up from being a puppy, held a special fondness and regard for him.

Now, it has to be said, that whenever we visited relatives or friends and Jack happened to be with us, the first thing he would do, once he had gained entrance inside a house, was to search it. Even before our hosts had been given the opportunity to welcome him into their home, he would start on the upper level by racing up the stairs. We would then listen to the patter of his paws as he went from each of the rooms, searching and scrutinising.

When he returned to us, he would then veer off to inspect each room on the ground floor, until finally he would settle down and remain motionless until it was time to leave. Odd behaviour for any dog? Absolutely, but how could you not smile at such characteristic capers and stand back in complete surprise, wondering whatever would come next?

On one of the days he went on his early morning walk with me to fetch the newspapers, I rejoined him at his usual tethering post, and began the walk past other shops towards home. When we reached a Ladies Hair Salon, just down from the newsagents, I met up with an old friend who was the local window cleaner and a keen football supporter. We stood and discussed many aspects of the previous Saturday's league games, and whilst doing so, I didn't notice the end of the lead I was holding had carelessly slipped from my grasp.

As I was about to say goodbye to my friend, I

turned and only then realised, Jack had disappeared. At the same time there were a number of excited screams coming from women inside the salon.

Quickly I entered through the open door only to be confronted by one of the girls working there, who frantically explained that there was a Jack Russell Terrier upstairs where the customers sat beneath hair dryers, chasing around and running under the ladies legs, as if out of control

"It's okay," I told the girl, trying to reassure her, "All he's doing is being nosy and inspecting the premises."

She looked bewildered.

"He doesn't work for the Health and Safety people does he?" she jokingly remarked.

"He does it all the time," I continued, "It won't be long before he comes chasing down those stairs to report back."

As I spoke, down he came, dragging his lead behind him, with vociferous protests and good humoured comments, coming from the upper level. Jack had put the fear of Christ into those ladies upstairs, and when he came back to me with his tail wagging, I snatched his lead before he could commence, what would have been, his intended search of the ground floor.

He became the talk of that salon for weeks to come, and my mate who I had been discussing the current state of football with earlier, had remained to find out what all the fuss had been about.

"Well, there's one thing," he remarked, "At least it wasn't a barber's shop he invaded, which shows he prefers women to men."

During that same hot summer, Richard the farmer came to me in a state of anxiety. The sheep required shearing, and the problem he had was the generator they used to feed power to the shears back at the farm, had gone down, and it would be weeks before he and his four sons who ran the farm, could get a replacement. In the meantime, the flock with their heavy woollen coats would suffer from the heat of the sun.

"Is there any way you can help, John?" he asked.

Without hesitation, of course I agreed to ease the situation and suggested the farmer could run a line from my garage into the field, and do the shearing on the other side of the hedge. But there was one condition, which I knew, Richard would immediately agree to and in fact, encourage. I suggested it would be an opportunity for the kids on our small estate to actually witness the shearing of sheep, as it actually took place.

So, we decided to undertake the necessary task on a late afternoon, when the temperature got cooler. With some help from Richard's four sons and a couple of labourers, a number of wooden stands were erected just inside the field, and various portable open cages were constructed in which it was intended to hold the sheep, prior to having their burdens removed.

In the meantime, we publicised the event by inviting all the families in the neighbourhood to attend, and on the day in question, there was a large gathering of children and their parents, all congregated on the field side of our hedge, waiting in anticipation of the main event.

Jack was in awe of what was going on, and sat near to where I stood, watching the men as they wired up the leads coming from the individual electric shears in readiness. There were six stands in total, which meant six sheep could be dealt with at any given time, a God send when we were looking at over two hundred woollies to be shorn.

The work began, with six shearers grabbing a Ewe each and quickly getting to work. Each coat of wool was transferred and loaded into the back of a large truck, and the onlookers retained a fascinated interest in the proceedings.

On each occasion a Ewe was taken to a shearer, Jack barked once, as if to tell the shearer that he had another one to deal with. This went on throughout the whole operation, until eventually, the children were laughing and paying more attention to Jack's solo barks, than to the other entertainment.

Once he recognised he was now becoming the

centre of attention, he decided to make it two barks for each of the sheep, glancing at his audience after each effort and wagging his tail.

After the work had been completed, old Richard came up to us, and patted Jack on the head, asking, "How many sheep did we do, Jack?"

He then turned to me, and admitted, "I could have sworn he was keeping count for us."

That following Christmas, we received some gifts of appreciation from the farmers, including a packet of treats for the little dog who had kept everyone entertained throughout the shearing operation. He was most appreciative.

Chapter Five

The Fight Game

Apart from the occasion he had gone missing in Lozells at a time when Jack was very young, the greatest fear I had for my companion's personal safety came one late autumn afternoon. We were enjoying our usual romp down by a narrow stream which divided one large fairly flat field, with another, which had an incline. The hillside contained within its boundary lines, a small copse of tall trees, which was in need of investigation. So, we crossed over a small wooden bridge and entered the upper field through a gate, with Jack leading the way in his usual enthusiastic manner.

After a great deal of sniffing amongst the fallen leaves, and searching the undergrowth covering the ground within the copse, the light was beginning to fade and a chill was in the air. It was time to go home, and I retraced my footsteps with my dog following behind. But rather than walk directly up the centre of the field adjacent to our home, I decided to make a small detour, intending to take Jack up a narrow lane which gave access to a local quarry.

When we arrived through yet another gate, at the bottom of the lane, and close to the back entrance to the quarry, there was a fairly high, built up bank of trees and bracken on one side.

Just as I turned to begin making my way homeward up the lane, there it was, standing motionless, staring down at both of us from the top of the embankment. A large wild cat with pointed ears.

I froze on the spot, not quite believing what I was witnessing. Although, the observer was showing no signs of aggression, it was watching our every movement through some of the thick bracken, and I wasn't fooled by the apparent cat's impassivity. The potential danger was undoubtedly targeting the dog.

Quickly, I stepped across towards Jack, who was busy putting his wet nose to good use around the base of a gate post, intending to get the lead on him, just in case the cat decided he would be easy prey. But before I could secure him, he looked up and began to growl, before invading the surrounding silence with a bout of fierce barking. He had seen the danger, and was determined to take control.

My only thought at that time was for the safety of the dog, and yet before I could stop him in his tracks, Jack quickly ran across my path, towards the bottom of the bank upon which the cat was still standing, unmoved. What I suspected was a Lynx, just remained inanimate, its eyes now focused on the white terrier, crawling towards it through the bracken.

I shouted at Jack to stand, but was completely ignored. There was nothing I could do to prevent what was to be a certain confrontation, which would in all probability see the end of my dog's life. But Jack was in-errantly climbing up that incline, with all the hostility he could muster, obviously prepared to take on his adversary head on, in a gladiatorial manner. It would be an act of suicidal proportions.

When he thought the distance between himself and the Lynx was optimal for him to launch his attack, the growling was replaced by more barking, as he stood from the ground, in readiness for the combat to begin.

Thankfully, the prelude to the contest must have had an adverse effect on the wild cat, which suddenly turned and retreated over the top of the embankment. Such a withdrawal only triggered more determination in Jack to attack, and he too, disappeared from sight, after thrashing his way through the undergrowth, hot on his target's heels.

My only concern then was if that Lynx decided to turn and fight, my dog would undoubtedly be torn apart, like a piece of paper going through a shredder. I kept shouting at him to return to heel, but might just as well have been a thousand miles away, for what impact my words had on my Jack Russell Terrier.

In fear of my dog being subjected to the most gruesome and painful injuries imaginable, I hastily thrashed my own path through the bracken, until I reached the top of the mound, beyond which there was a field containing a number of horses. I grasped my walking stick in readiness to defend my four legged companion, but there was no need. Never before had I been so relieved to see him skipping jauntily back towards me, wagging his tail. There was no sign of the Lynx.

Thankfully, he was fine and looked inquisitively at me, as if asking what all the fuss was about. I stood for a moment, still scanning the terrain in search of any sign of that cat, but it had vacated the area, as quickly as it had made its presence known earlier.

"Don't you ever ignore me like that again, you crazy mutt," I called to him in chastisement, but my words fell on deaf ears, and he just stood there with his tongue hanging out, looking around.

Once I had the lead on him, and we had both returned to the lane below, I felt more at ease, and both man and dog made their way towards home in the greyness of the autumn dusk. However, I couldn't help but keep looking back over my shoulder, just in case that wild cat had a notion to stalk us, but we never encountered it ever again, for which I was thankful.

I must admit to feeling some sympathy for the cat, realising the animal must have been starving, and very frightened by the audacity of this doughty and noisily aggressive canine creature.

I reported the sighting to a friend who was a reporter at a local newspaper, and was told there had been several sightings of the Lynx in the area, which didn't really surprise me. Anyway, it so happened, that following that nerve biting incident, on each occasion I took the dog out on the fields, I carried a starting pistol with me, just in case, but there was no need. That took place some five years ago, and there have been no further sightings of the wild cat since.

Whether it was his success at scaring off such a stronger adversary, I'm not sure, but I did notice a definite change in Jack's attitude following that incident, especially when he confronted other dogs, in particular, breeds that were much bigger than him in size.

Shortly after the meeting with the wild cat, we were standing at our garden gate, when we met a friend who owned an English Bull Terrier called 'Stewie'. It was a rescue dog that suffered from total deafness, but lived for chasing a ball across the fields. Whenever we had met the couple previously, Stewie would drop his ball at my feet, begging for it to be thrown, so he could chase it and bring it back for a repeat performance. He had a wonderful and friendly temperament, and when ever I had the opportunity, I would oblige the Bull Terrier by participating in his games.

Well, on this occasion, Jack was at my side, staring at Stewie through the wooden struts of the gate. Then it happened. The playful Bull Terrier decided to stick its nose through the gate itself, with Jack standing there, watching the audacious encroachment on his territory.

It was a blatant trespass and my dog went berserk, barking and snapping at the other dog, but Stewie was in no mood to be dictated to by some yapping Jack Russell Terrier, and suddenly snapped back, taking a piece of flesh off the top of Jack's nose. The result was only a surface wound, but sufficient for, Jack to remain extremely quiet for days to come. He sulked and kept his head hanging low, showing no desire to leave the house, until the lesion on his snout had disappeared.

The wound which was kept clean and dry, soon healed without leaving any trace, but following that incident, whenever we met up with our friend and her English Bull Terrier, Jack was kept on a leash, not withstanding he hadn't learnt his lesson and was still willing to get his own back, each time Stewie came into his vision.

A third incident took place shortly after the wound inflicted on Jack had healed. A close friend and business associate had another Jack Russell

Terrier, and whilst discussing business at her home, we decided to take the two dogs for a walk, which took us across a motorway pedestrian bridge into some fields on the other side.

Eventually, we reached a small pond, and allowed the dogs off the leads to play about in the water. That was a mistake, and there was a sudden outburst of hostility, as both dogs rolled about on the grass, locked in mortal combat.

I had to lever Jack off the other dog, whose name was, Muppet, and it was obvious that, Muppet was a little upset at having the fight brought to a premature end, before he'd had chance to prove himself against his opponent.

We immediately walked them back to my friend's house, both secured on their leads; both still growling at each other, but both dogs kept distanced from each other. By the time we returned to our destination, I was ready to return home.

Muppet was taken inside the house, whilst I picked Jack up, to place him in the back of the car. But before I could do so, and still holding my dog in my arms, Muppet suddenly came chasing out of the house, barking out a war cry before leaping at Jack, who was helplessly vulnerable and restrained in my arms. Fortunately, I managed to heave Jack up well out of reach of the snapping jaws, and a frustrated, Muppet was admonished and returned to the interior of the house, obviously disillusioned at having missed a wonderful opportunity to get the better of his adversary.

From that time onward, each time I visited my associate's house, Jack was left in the car, until I was ready to return home.

There were other occasions when my dog

decided to go into battle with other dogs, and I remained wary when taking him for romps across the fields. As soon as another dog came into sight, on the lead he would go, until the danger had passed.

I remember on one occasion, two ladies were walking their black Labrador dog down by the stream. They obviously believed in social networking amongst canines, and were encouraging Jack to meet up with their dog. I knew at the time, there would only be one outcome should that meeting take place, so decided to tell the ladies a little white lie. I advised them that Jack had a contagious disease amongst dogs, and was having treatment at the vets.

As if fleeing from the Blitz, both ladies quickly scurried away, with their dog being hastily dragged behind them on a lead. At least, I believed I had avoided what would have undoubtedly been a hugely embarrassing and violent confrontation.

I quickly discovered that Jack's aversion towards other dogs, was aimed solely towards those that were bigger in size than himself, and which he obviously looked upon as being a threat. Bitches were never a problem, and whenever we met up with other canines on our pedestrian travels, I would hold back until ascertaining the sex of other dogs, before allowing him off the lead.

One particular bitch he seemed to get on well with, was a Yorkshire Terrier, we later found out was named Millie. It became a frequent occurrence for the little Yorkie to suddenly appear in our back garden, and would spend lengthy periods running about over the lawn, with Jack chasing her.

Finally, I found the way in which, Millie was entering our garden, through a small hole in the hedge, which I eventually blocked. I had no idea of who the owner of the Yorkie bitch was, only that she lived somewhere locally. Anyway, after a short time, she stopped visiting and Jack showed no signs of missing her.

A few months later, our son, Neil came home and reported he had seen a small number of puppies in the kitchen of a lady's house in the village. According to, Neil they were all exact replicas of Jack, and he noticed their mother, who was sitting watching over her pups, was none other than Millie the Yorkshire Terrier. Well done Father Jack.

The one principle part of Jack's character was his sense of pain, or rather his lack of it. Rarely have I heard him squeal out in discomfort, or complain when injured as a result of some small accident that had befallen him. Even when visiting the vets for various inoculations, not a murmur would be heard when the needle was plunged into his neck. Only on one occasion can I recall him moaning about his predicament, and that was following an operation to which he was subjected to.

An example of his reluctance to communicate any pain he was feeling, was when he was young, and I took him for a lengthy walk around the outskirts of the village where we lived. He was on the lead and was happily enjoying his walk, when suddenly he stopped and raised a paw. So I picked him up from the pavement and quickly saw a small spike of metal protruding from the pad of one of his front paws.

He just looked at me in anticipation, and in

response I just said, "This has to come out, Jack and without any delay."

I then took hold of the spike and pulled it out, with a trickle of blood following the object. Yet, at no time did he make a murmur, although he was carried for the rest of the short journey. Such was this little dog's resilience to pain, and one of the reasons I felt so emotionally attached to him. If ever there was a dog with a huge pain barrier, it was my four legged companion.

Ready to start his new life

Playtime   *Meeting with the lambs*

No fear of water

After his fight with a Bull Terrier

The Meriden Fire

Ready for the next romp

Exploring the open fields

Bath time

Taking a break   *Adventure at every turn*

Chapter Six

The Hero

When exploring the open countryside, we always took advantage of what daylight was left, and would remain out of doors until being finally forced to return home, before the darkness of night overtook us. On occasions we would be so engrossed in some natural feature, such as a centuries old gnarled oak, or rare bird sitting on top of a fence, resting, that before we realised it, the dusk would be rapidly closing in on us. There were a number of times when, by the time we actually returned home, the full darkness of night had fallen.

Following his numerous bouts of conflict with other dogs well met, and which didn't quite fit into Jack's selection procedures, yet another curious incident occurred which propelled him once again, into the media.

It was fairly late one spring evening and we needed to return home before the light faded altogether. We had been skirting a perimeter fence around a large quarry near our home. It was an unusual site in that great holes dug out of the landscape for the recovery of sand used in the building industry, had filled with water, forming miniature lakes upon which rare species of birds had made their homes. In fact, so many different and rare species had appeared and nested inside the quarry boundaries, there were a number of various protection and prohibition orders in place. It naturally soon followed that the area became a magnet for bird watchers, who would be occasionally seen armed with both binoculars and cameras.

In a large copse of trees adjacent to the quarry, some of the rare birds had made permanent homes, so that too, was protected. I often saw Grouse, Pheasant and Partridge roaming around the area, and the sight of a hawk gliding on the wing was fairly common. A Cuckoo could often be heard within that particular confine, and at night the constant hooting of an Owl would echo across the nearby countryside. That particular patch of protected land also benefitted from a small complex belonging to the local Water Board, which had filter beds and was regularly attended, preventing any unwanted intruders from getting close to, and disturbing the birds.

On one side of the quarry, which looked out on to the open fields, there was a man-made grassed over ridge, built to hide the quarry workings from any grazing land or enthusiastic walkers. The small lakes contained within the facility were in an ideal location for non-interference, and we would often walk down there to quietly observe the natural peaceful habitat of the birds and wild fowl. With high mounds of sand and gravel surrounding each of the man-made lakes, the whole scene was similar to one you could associate with, Lawrence of Arabia.

As I have mentioned previously, the area was frequently visited by bird watchers, who on occasions would approach me, asking if I had caught any sighting of some rare specimen, the name of which I could never repeat and was usually beyond my abilities of pronunciation.

Sometimes an enthusiast would enquire as to how they could gain access to the perimeter of the quarry and, although most access points were extremely hazardous, I would share with them the safest route to an unobstructed viewing stage, from which they could see the whole vista.

Whenever such a chance meeting took place, Jack would stand back and observe the bird watcher with a hint of suspicion, and on occasions, individuals would make a hasty retreat when the dog, for whatever reason, would let out a growl of unacceptability.

"It's okay," I used to shout after them, feeling a little embarrassed by his hostility, "His growls are bigger than his bite," but I cannot recall any of them accepting my word.

For my part, I thought it right that people who visited the countryside for all the right reasons, should be made welcome and encouraged as much as possible. Sometimes, not just bird watchers would approach us, but hikers who were confused by their map readings. Many a time, I have had to put them back on the right path, to reach their intended destination, and, as if Jack favoured hikers more than other visitors to our domain, he would always allow those with heavy packs on their backs, to stroke him without objection.

We were walking across the field that was immediately adjacent to the ridge that helped to hide the quarry workings from prying eyes. The lambing season had just finished and prancing lambs could be seen in almost every field within sight.

When we neared the grassed over ridge, my four legged companion suddenly raised his head and stood for a moment, obviously trying to determine something which had drawn his attention. Most of the time he was chasing around the open countryside, his nose would be glued to the ground, assessing every different smell and wild plant he came across. So, when he became alerted to whatever it was, so did I, and watched from a distance, as he bolted through a hole in a wire fence. Flying past various warning signs of danger, he climbed up the incline, before disappearing over the top of the ridge, into the quarry itself.

I loudly called for him to return, and he quickly re-appeared, standing for a moment with both ears up, and barking back at me, before once again disappearing from sight down the other side. He repeated this course of action several times, appearing at the top of the ridge, barking for attention, before once again doing his vanishing trick.

Finally, with the dusk rapidly approaching, I sensed that there was something woeful, which had caused him to behave in such a manner, so quickly made my own way up the same incline to the very top, hoping it wasn't another wild cat. There on the other side, which opened up to the scenic portrait of the miniature lakes, stood Jack, again yapping with all his might, and staring across at a lamb, which was obviously stuck in the wet sand that surrounded the nearest water.

I told the dog to stay put and cautiously approached the distressed lamb, which was surrounded by extremely precarious and unstable ground. I had to move gingerly, not wanting to become entrapped in a similar fashion to the casualty. Each light footstep I took sank down into the wet sand, but somehow managed to hold my weight, although the closer I got to the distressed lamb, the further my boots sank into the ground.

Finally I reached a very distraught youngster, who was frantically trying to escape from the clutches of the demanding sandbank, which identified the problem. The more the lamb struggled, the deeper it went into the mire. Carefully I bent down and managed to lift the protesting lamb from its confinement, not realising until that time, just how heavy a lamb of two months, weighed.

Thankfully, once our distraught little friend was in my arms, it stopped struggling, as if knowing what we were doing was for its benefit. Eventually, with an overjoyed Jack following at my heels, I managed to return to the safety of the ridge, but knew without its mother, that lamb would probably perish. So, we both persevered, with me holding on to the casualty, until we finally got back to the field below.

Each lamb had a number painted on its side, which corresponded with the same number displayed on its mother. The one I was struggling with bore the number five, and the next phase of the rescue was to find the Ewe with the same number.

After searching through the flock, we managed to find her grazing down by a stream. The Ewe looked up and eyed us warily, moving towards her offspring, which was still in my arms. Slowly I lowered the lamb to the ground, relieved to shed my burden.

The reunion was immediate, and the bleating lamb ran to its mother's side, but there was no thanks offered. Instead, the Ewe sniffed her returned prodigal, before standing proud and stamping both of its front hooves on the ground in strong protest at our presence.

"What a bloody ungrateful sheep head," I said to Jack, who barked back in agreement.

But our good deed for that day had been accomplished, and Richard the farmer was extremely appreciative, when I later reported the incident to him.

For Jack's part he immediately became a hero, and thanks to the farmer's enthusiasm to share the story around the village, the local newspaper wrote up a short article on the dog's endeavours. Once again, I felt extremely proud of my four legged friend for a long time after the incident, and extra portions of biscuits were placed in his dish.

It was shortly after the incident involving the trapped lamb, that Jack, yet again, confirmed his natural and amazing sense of danger. It was late at night, when he began to alert us to an existing problem coming from the fields. He suddenly went to the back door and began to bark, which was indeed a rarity, and usually reserved for strangers approaching the house, or neighbours visiting. Even if he sensed a rat close by to the house, he would still make for the back door, but remain silent, as if not wanting to alert that which he intended to kill, but on this occasion, I knew it wasn't a rat that had attracted his attention.

After placing him on the lead, we both walked down the garden in the darkness, until we reached the gate. Looking across the fields, I could see in the distance, where the quarry was situated, an orange glow in the sky. Then flames began to appear on the horizon, leaping upwards to the night sky, and owing to the distance between where we stood, and where the fire was located, I realised it was no small deal.

After phoning for the Fire Brigade and giving them the location of the inferno, I walked Jack up to a top gate, which gave access to the same narrow lane, not far from where we had come across the wild cat previously. But from there, we could get a better view of the fire itself. It seemed that the whole quarry was alight, and there was a real danger that if it spread across the dividing ridge, it could be possibly present a danger to the sheep grazing on our side of the facility. Of course, further danger was presented to the numerous rare birds and fowl that had made their home inside the quarry, resulting in a lot of concern for their safety.

The next step was to inform the farmer of the situation, and as blue flashing lights of fire engines could be seen entering the quarry from the far side, Richard kept a close vigil on his stock. He decided there was no immediate danger to the sheep, but we still maintained a watch over that fire, until the flames began to subside after half the night had passed by, with fire fighters, trying to gain control over the perilous situation.

The following morning, clouds of acrid smoke were still filling the air around where the fire had occurred, and we met one of the fire fighters who informed us of what had actually happened. It transpired that people had been using the quarry to pile their rubbish, so much so, that a vast amount of public waste had collected on site. It was that which had caught alight. Fortunately the Fire Brigade had managed to contain the problem, and the feathered occupants inside the confine had remained safe.

Amazingly, the Fire Fighters remained present for a number of days, amongst the smoking hot rubble, before they finally managed to dampen the ground sufficiently to be safe.

What I took from that incident, was the phenomenal way in which, Jack had sensed the danger initially. It seemed that his natural abilities held no boundary, and once again, the extra portions of biscuits were distributed.

By now, Meriden Jack had been widely recognised as being a special little dog, but my own opinion of my closest companion was that he was extremely wary, intelligent, and the closest I had ever known to being human. He sought no recognition for his achievements; no fuss or additional compliment or celebration. In fact, Jack was quite the opposite, rejecting fuss of any kind, or appreciation bestowed upon him by well meaning individuals, other than myself. He was the kind of dog that leapt from one adventurous crisis to another, not stopping or seeking any accolades. And it was that part of his character that made me pleased and extremely proud to know him.

Chapter Seven

Disaster with the Media

By the time Jack was reaching full maturity, he had already become a one dog audience and cemented his position as a constant observer in my study, whenever I was engaged with my work. One of his many talents developed further during our country runs, was his ability to scale tall obstacles, and on occasions when he was impatient to wait for a gate to be opened, he would just leap over the fence. Therefore, his habit of jumping on top of my desk, to either spend time watching me at the computer, or just dozing off, was no big deal for him. Whenever I was ready to take a break, he would always be ready in attendance to lead the way for yet another outdoor frolic.

I recall, during a period I was writing a feature page for the Sunday Mercury newspaper, an appointment had been made to interview an interesting chap who lived in a converted barn outside Lichfield. The subject of that week's story was a former cricketing umpire who had been involved in travelling the world to seek the Holy Grail, and already having been responsible for uncovering two of them, he believed there existed a third, and was preparing to go in search of that final chalice. The content of the story was both unusual and fascinating, so I was looking forward to the interview.

It was a hot sunny day, when I pulled up in a yard which led to my intended interviewee's accommodation, and as usual, my four legged companion was in attendance. I was early and it would be another half an hour before my photographer would arrive, but I decided to get on with the interview.

"I love dogs," my host announced, standing by his front door to welcome me, "You can bring him in with you if you so wish."

I had intended in leaving Jack secured in some shady spot, not wanting to leave him inside the car, especially in that heat, and appreciated the invitation. So did Jack, as I opened the car door to allow him to leap out. But, mischief being his middle name, as soon as he had regained his freedom, he ran in front of me, heading directly towards the same man who was the reason I was there. For the briefest of moments, I thought my dog was going to thank the man by leaping up at him, but Jack had other ideas.

The dog ran past the man, before suddenly leaving the ground, and dramatically launching himself over an eight foot wooden fence that stood behind my host, who couldn't quite believe what he was seeing. Jack disappeared from sight over the other side, leaving me to once again, apologise for having a pet with so much impish roguery in his character.

The man nervously laughed, but was as obviously surprised as I was, and quickly explained that there was a canal on the other side of the fence behind which Jack had vaulted over.

He gave me a leg up and I grasped the top of the fence, only to see that my dog had avoided falling into the water, and was in fact, sitting on the narrow towpath, looking up at me. The problem Jack had, was from that side of the fence, he had insufficient room to run before leaping back.

"What are you?" I called out, beckoning him to do what he could, to reach my outstretched hands.

He knew exactly what I was suggesting and managed to scratch his way up the far side of the fence, until I was able to grab a hold of him, and hoist him back up over the fence.

"I've never seen anything like that before," my host confessed.

"Not many have," I confirmed. But that was Jack the Terrier, a day never passing by without some surprise package coming from my dog.

When the photographer arrived, the subject of the interview explained what the dog had done.

"That's nothing," my colleague confirmed, "I once saw him jump over a sheep's back on all fours, just like a pole vaulter but without the pole."

"Did you take his picture?" the man asked.

"No chance. I pleaded with him, but he wouldn't do it again."

Like all publishers in those days, my own was a stalwart for obtaining as much publicity as he could solicit, each time a new novel was published. Following each book launch, a barrage of media interviews would follow with press, television or radio. It was all good fun, although when long journeys were involved, especially when having to travel down to London, and spend a great deal of time involved in various interviews at designated radio stations, or at glossy magazine offices, exhaustion did occasionally tend to kick in. There were also numerous presentations arranged at different major book stores across the United Kingdom, and little time was made available for sight seeing.

Initially, and particularly before, Jack came along, I used to thoroughly enjoy undertaking a commitment north of the border, in Edinburgh or Glasgow, where many of the launches and presentations were accompanied by whiskey tasting events. However, such trips would mean being away from home for up to a week or more.

Whenever, I returned from such contractual commitments, Jack would always be up at the front window, no matter what time, day or night, I presented myself. As soon as he would see the car, or taxi, he would instantly start barking to inform everyone else I had come home, at the same time racing to the back door to await my entrance into the house. That dog would never allow me further than the back door, until he had displayed his greetings by lying flat on his back, or running rings around my feet. He certainly evidenced the fact he had missed me.

On one occasion when I was involved in a business trip to Lyon in France, I was absent for just five days, and one evening I rang my wife to ascertain that all was well at home. She laughingly informed me that on each night since I had left for the Continent, the dog had climbed onto the bed and had sat there, howling himself to sleep. Well, such news brought me a feeling of some satisfaction, knowing that my absence was being recognised in such a canine way, but I became concerned that Jack could be grieving, which would not be to his benefit, and couldn't wait to return home following that conversation.

There were a few occasions when I was able to drive to a book launch, rather than fly or be taxied, and would take my close companion with me. I must admit, having to stop frequently to exercise and water him became a chore, which now and then resulted in me being late for an appointment. But everyone who met Jack, soon forgot about my own failing, and he would quickly become the centre of attention. Eventually, I had to decide on whether to leave him at home, or risk disharmony with a time schedule. I rejected both options and it was agreed for me to complete most of my media work at home.

On one occasion, a reporter and film crew travelled from Manchester to Meriden to record an interview for Granada Television. After completing the project, the female reporter was admiring the scenery at the back of the house, when she suddenly had an idea, and asked if it was possible to film, Jack running across the open field.

Of course I agreed, and the camera was set up in the back garden, during the time it took me to escort my four legged companion down the field for a couple of hundred yards. In compliance with the directions given to me, I called Jack to my side and we both slowly walked back towards the house, with Jack's snout on the ground, and the camera rolling.

The reporter was thrilled, and just before the program went out on Granada Television, she sent me the usual copy tape. My one to one interview was shown for about three minutes of air time. Jack's walk across the fields, which included close ups of the dog, lasted for twice as long.

"You my friend, are a true star," I told him, but

he just continued rolling across the floor, panting and stretching out his legs.

Whenever we filmed at my home, Jack was always sent to the kitchen with the door closed, to avoid the sound engineer from being interrupted by any sudden yapping. Occasionally, we would be halfway through an interview, when there would be a sudden outburst of barking from the kitchen, and we would have to start the filming all over again.

As time passed by, and Jack became accustomed to all of these people visiting at the same time, carrying all kinds of equipment, cameras and microphones, he finally understood that making his presence known wasn't exactly the thing to do. That was until, my little friend took it upon himself to cause, what could only be described as a humongous and embarrassing disaster.

I had agreed to take part in a live show for the Midlands Today programme, which was intended to support a newly published book with a great deal of focus targeting the subject matter I had written.

Kate, the Marketing Director from my Publishing House, travelled up from London to keep an eye on things, and ensure that all went well.

During the evening of the live interview, it must have taken a good hour for the television engineers and designated reporter to set things up. The usual large communications van was parked outside the front of the house, with an extended satellite dish protruding through its roof. Cables were run from the van into the front lounge, where the camera and microphones were carefully positioned. Windows were blacked out and lights switched on. Finally, the news reporter took his seat opposite where I sat, with various wires and leads coming from most parts of my anatomy. At last, everyone was ready for the live broadcast to begin.

As the countdown began, I spent a couple of minutes talking with the studio presenters, Nick Owen and Suzanne Verdi, about other subjects unconnected with the program. A voice was heard confirming we had two minutes to broadcast. Then the one minute warning was given, and we all steeled ourselves in readiness for the off. Then it happened; surprisingly and unexpectedly, everything crashed before we had even gone on air.

The lighting went down and the mains power to the camera disappeared. There was both confusion and panic. Mobile phones were produced and calls made to the studio back at Pebble Mill. My front lounge was quickly thrown into complete turmoil. Then one of the engineers came striding in and called out, "He's cut the bloody mains cable."

We all simultaneously asked, "Who?"

Somehow, Jack had quietly managed to escape from the kitchen, obviously taking advantage of the front door being left open to accommodate all the cables leading into the house. I could only assume he became fascinated by this strange vehicle parked outside the front, which resembled a wagon belonging to NASA, and decided to go for an investigative rummage.

According to witnesses, he'd actually jumped up into the back of the van, and again, I can only guess that being attracted by the colour of the yellow mains cable, decided to taste it. The dog had bitten straight through the main cable, just as we were about to go live on the air. Well, everything turned blue, and a few mild altercations took place, with me defending my dog and issuing a few threats to anyone who even had the slightest inclination of chastising him.

Eventually, it was decided we would record the intended interview, and a motor cyclist was dispatched to pick up the tape and speedily get it back to the studio. Instead of there being a live interview at the beginning of the show, there was a recorded version at the end, and Jack was confined back to the kitchen, for his own safety.

Obviously, I offered my apologies for the minor disaster, but after all, when a Jack Russell is on the loose, who has a constant thirst for adventure and mischief, what are you doing leaving the door to a van full of electrical equipment, open? Well, that was my excuse for my four legged mutt, and we both stood our ground.

Eventually, when I later met both Nick and Suzanne at their new headquarters at the Mail Box in Birmingham, all three of us laughed the incident off. But I'm not so sure the show's producer would have found it so funny. And yet, if that particular incident was deemed to be traumatic as well as catastrophic, there was much more to come a little later, with compliments from Jack.

Chapter Eight

A close tie

The Czech born French writer, Milan Kundera, once wrote, 'Dogs are our link to paradise. They don't know evil or jealousy or discontent. To sit with a dog on a hillside on a glorious afternoon is to be back in Eden, where doing nothing was not boring – it was peace'.

How many times have I tried to explain to other dog owners that their pet possessed no animosity, or feelings of personal rejection when words spoken to it would be an affront to human beings? It was a lesson I quickly learned during the years I have been proud to be Jack's principle companion, and I also know that when he has finally gone, where ever he will be buried won't matter, because in truth he will be buried in my heart. Such is the deep emotional relationship I have enjoyed with a small dog that has been no angel, but has certainly been brave and courageous, and above all, extremely loyal, not once asking for anything in return.

I believe it was the famous heart transplant surgeon, Christian Barnard, who once said that pet dogs were therapeutic. I would venture to go beyond that description, and suggest that, yes, they can be therapeutic, but they also offer much unconditional love and at times, unexpected motivation. Many a time, I have sat on that hillside, mentioned by, Milan Kundera, basking in the sun and enjoying a peaceful existence, whilst watching my dog, achieving great happiness by running, walking and exploring adventurously, close by.

The only time I have known, Jack become concerned, was when I would walk out of the door and he wasn't sure that I was ever going to return. That was the case on the day of our daughter, Jo's wedding to her future husband, Adam.

Of course I would be attending the wedding as the father of the bride, fully committed to fulfilling my ceremonial obligations. Such was never in doubt, but the problem presented to us, was that the marriage was to take place in the rural countryside of Worcestershire, which was quite a distance from where we lived. Under normal circumstances, no difficulty would exist, but now, there was a Parson Jack Russell Terrier to take into consideration. The occasion would mean that, Jack would have to be left for a considerable length of time, inducing a number of options which needed careful consideration.

Because I was well aware of the dog's temperament, I had always been extremely reluctant to leave him as a boarder, even if only for a day or two. Therefore, when plans were being made for the big occasion, the question of what we would do with Jack, came up for discussion on several occasions.

I was obstinately adamant, he should be cared for by a friend, if possible, rather than be confined in some kennel and tended by complete strangers. But what friend was there, who had become close enough for Jack to remain with?

Eventually, understanding the dilemma I was

experiencing, my business partner, Ellie, who had also known, Jack since he was a puppy, kindly agreed to look after him throughout the day of the forthcoming celebration. Having secured Ellie's valued assistance, we then devised a plan intended to keep the amount of time my associate would be virtually lumbered with my dog's presence, to a bare minimum. We decided that my absence would only be for that one day, which at the time appeared reasonable. After all, Jack couldn't have it all his way, and to miss his romps across the fields for just that singular day, couldn't surely present any problems. Or could it?

So, it came to pass that my wife, Ann, was to stay with our daughter at the hotel where the reception was to be held, to help in whatever way she could. Following the ceremony and post wedding reception, she would again, remain overnight at the same hotel, in the company of her sister, Marie.

For my part, I was to remain at home with Jack, until the early morning of the wedding. Then on my way to the same hotel, I was to call at, Ellie's house and leave the dog there, intending to collect him on the same night, once the celebrations had come to an end. I would then take him home and remain with him throughout that night, before returning the following morning. It seemed to be a logical and full proof plan, and I was overjoyed that we had finally come up with a solution, thanks to my business partner.

When the big day finally arrived, before leaving the house, Jack was brushed and combed and even had his teeth cleaned. He looked quite prim and proper, as he leapt into the back of the car, obviously looking forward to his next adventure. I could only hope he saw it as just that.

On the way to the hotel in Worcestershire, I called at Ellie's home, remaining for only a couple of minutes, to make sure that Jack was settled. He just sat there, calm and allowing his minder for the day to make a fuss of him. When the first opportunity came, I left him sitting in the hallway, next to the front door, and deliberately ignored him, as I quietly and surreptitiously disappeared from sight, before heading for the hotel where the rest of the family would be gathered.

The sun shone and a cloudless sky remained with us throughout a day in which all appeared to go without any hitch. I proudly accomplished my tasks as father of the bride with all the enthusiasm and panache I could muster. It was indeed a joyous occasion for all in attendance, and our hearts and well wishes went out to Jo and Adam.

The evening celebrations also went well, and friends and family members intermingled with each other, all sharing the happiness of the bride and groom. I enjoyed much of the reminiscing that was shared, and remained for as long as I dared. Finally, when it came time to leave and collect Jack from Ellie's house, I firstly made arrangements to return the following morning in time for breakfast at the hotel. My daughter and her new husband would still be there, before leaving for their honeymoon, so I would be able to bid them farewell, and a safe journey before they departed.

As I drove through the dark and quiet lanes of Worcestershire, heading for the motorway, it was gone past eleven o'clock, so I phoned Ellie to inform her I was on my way to collect my four legged companion. Well, I was shocked by the news that greeted me. In fact, I had to stop the car and park up, in order to take account of the story she had shared with me, describing her nightmarish day with my Jack Russell Terrier.

After leaving him on that morning, he had remained by the front door for a couple of hours, without any untoward incident. Apparently, he allowed people to fuss him, and appeared to be well settled. Then, according to his minder, it was as if he had just realised for the first time that I was absent, and had been for some time. Not knowing where I had disappeared to, he became extremely restless and aggressive, and his temperament towards everybody present, changed quite dramatically.

Growling and showing his teeth to anyone who went near to him inside that hallway, Jack maintained a guard dog's vigil, without moving away from that front door for the rest of the day and evening. It was as though he had been given the task to protect that front door at all costs.

Ellie's brother was bitten whilst trying to pacify the dog, albeit only slightly, and her nephew, who also tried to reassure Jack, was quickly dispensed with by a frontal attack, which fortunately left him without injury, but not through any lack of canine intention.

At the time of my phone call to Ellie, she was alone in the house, locked inside the ground floor toilet, and unable to exit because, Jack was standing on the other side of the door, growling and threatening to attack anything that moved. I was horrified and embarrassed upon hearing such a disastrous report, including the fact that he'd bitten his minder's toes as she sought the protection of the toilet door. The portrait relayed to me was one which reminded me of a Hammer Film

Production, where an uncontrollable man-eating beast was at large.

With all haste I accelerated away and within a few minutes, was pulling up outside the front of the besieged house, still unable to believe what I had been told earlier.

As I approached the front door, the hallway lights were switched on, and I could see the outline of Jack, standing nearby, just inside, and exactly where I had left him earlier that morning.

The small window to the ground floor toilet sprung open, and Ellie handed me the key to her front door, still unable to escape from her enforced confinement.

As soon as I entered the house, the tail began to wag, and the home coming was concluded with an excitable, Jack rolling around the floor. I quickly lifted him off the carpet and held him in both arms.

His whole character had reverted back to how it had been when we had last parted company.

Ellie quietly appeared from her confinement, and I stood there, listening to a repeat of my dog's fall from grace. The look in those big brown eyes of his, told me that he knew he was the subject of the narrative, and I could feel him shivering nervously, looking up at me with trepidation. The conversation was most definitely not in his favour.

Of course, I felt some shame about his behaviour, and was extremely disappointed that he had let the side down. I would never have dreamt that his behaviour would have been so disarming and aggressive.

Obviously I offered my deepest regret and apologies before placing, Jack in the car and driving home. When we arrived, he still appeared to be agitated, and I became concerned, so, although it was pitch black out on the fields, I took him for a short walk on the lead to try and calm him down, knowing he must have had a traumatic day, for which I could only blame myself. My concern then, was for my dog, and accepting that it had been my own absence that had triggered most of the trauma, felt sympathetic towards him.

Jack was initially confused when I moved his bed upstairs, after ensuring he'd had something to eat and drink, and intending for him to sleep that night in the same room as myself. I thought that was the right thing to do, considering the state of the dog, and his need for company throughout that night. There was an urgent need to rid him of whatever nightmare thoughts had been occupying his mind, and return him to a state of normality as soon as possible.

In the morning, Jack *was* back to normal, and a

bright, sunny day greeted us both. Following an initial early morning walk, we both returned to the wedding party at the hotel I had departed from the night before. When explaining to the others what had taken place at Ellie's house the day before, everyone was aghast.

After breakfast, the bride and groom said their farewells, before being taxied off to enjoy their honeymoon. A small group of us remained and went for a long walk through the grounds of the hotel, with Jack exploring the landscape with us. At least it appeared he had recuperated from his ordeal, and I could only hope that Ellie and her own family members had also done the same. As it happened, the dog was forgiven for his transgressions, but was treated with a great deal of wariness by the same family members, following his day of embarrassing hostility.

I also learned from that experience that my dog was quick to become emotionally upset when I was absent, but he also was just as quick to recover, if showed some care and understanding. I gave a great deal of consideration to what had taken place, and accepted that part of the reason for his transgressions, was embedded within his character.

If he had been more docile and approachable, I believe he would not have possessed the other characteristics he had so often displayed. Jack was both strong willed and obstinate. He was also sensitive, but fearless, and I still believe that if the aggression within him was removed, the other emotions that are more acceptable, would also have disappeared. In other words my assessment of him was that each part of his character, good or back, was integrally connected.

So, it transpired that Jack attended the wedding after all, even if it was on the day that followed the event.

Chapter Nine

The Fox

Having tarnished his reputation with such impishness and unacceptable behaviour at Ellie's house, Jack remained fairly quiet for the few days that followed, as if having realised he had blotted his copy book seriously, or was still recovering from his traumatic experience. I was hoping it was the former, but doubted that was the case. However, he was soon back to his usual energetic and friendly old self, continuing to explore the open countryside, keeping a watchful eye over our grandson, Charlie, and taking out the occasional rodent, before presenting the same as a gift on the back lawn of some unsuspecting neighbour. But then, a turn of events led us all to once again become totally dumbfounded by the character and mannerisms of this small dog, whose life seemed to be enriched with adventurous controversy of some kind or another.

It was during the winter of 2010 when, Jack suddenly turned maverick, disappearing for no more than an hour or so during the early evening, before eventually returning home. At first we became concerned, but I remained easy because there was a pattern to his behaviour. And yet, following a few repeats of his disappearing escapades, it was time to investigate where my companion was visiting at such a late hour, and always alone. The most favoured opinion was that he had found a bitch somewhere on heat, and yet my instincts were telling me, that was not the case.

My first reaction was to find out how my dog was escaping from the back garden. There had to be a gap somewhere in the fairly dense Hawthorn hedge, and after some perseverance I eventually found it, near to where the hedge joined a brick wall, marking the boundary of our property.

On the next occasion, Jack decided to disappear, I also left the house appropriately dressed for the cold winter winds, and armed with both a torch and thick pair of gloves. I made my way on to the fields, knowing that he shouldn't be difficult to find in the darkness, owing to his bright white coat. On one previous and particular night time excursion, when the ground was covered in snow, Jack had only to move a few yards away from me, and would instantly disappear into the back ground. That resulted in the supply of a bright coloured fluorescent coat, used only for our night time walks.

Anyway, I slowly skirted the first field, searching for the white coated apparition, which I anticipated would soon be seen sniffing the ground in his customary manner. Sadly there was no sign of Jack, until I had just about completed a full tour of the perimeter, and was standing beneath an Elm Tree towards the centre of the field. The self-appointed tourist suddenly appeared through the darkness, trotting along and making his way towards our back gate. I didn't call him, and just watched as he drew nearer to home, before stopping and making one final examination of a small patch of grass near to the Hawthorn hedge.

Then the realisation that my dog was not alone, hit me like an unseen missile. I remained motionless and blinked my eyes, not quite understanding or believing the scene with which I was confronted. There, walking at a close distance behind my dog was a large dog fox, watching over him like some kind of research veterinary, observing his every move.

I remained about fifty yards away under the cover of darkness, and initially fearing that he was about to be attacked. But foxes didn't attack dogs, or so I thought at the time. Also both dog and fox appeared unconcerned about each others presence. So, I continued to observe the couple, until Jack finally stopped near to his access point through which he could return into our back garden.

The fox just stood there continuing to watch over him, as the terrier eventually disappeared through the hedge.

I patiently remained where I stood, wanting to see if the fox also had the cheek to follow Jack into the back garden, but it didn't, and after a short period of time, the wild animal suddenly took off, with its head hung low. I watched as it followed the hedge further up the field before disappearing from sight altogether. And only then, did I venture home.

When I reached the gate, I could see Jack waiting patiently at the back door, and upon realising I was there, sprinted to me with his tail wagging. To say I was absolutely flabbergasted is an understatement, and I had no idea whether that meeting with the fox had been a first encounter, or whether the previous occasions he had gone missing, was a result of a dog and fox going for an evening walk together. The latter seemed to be too incredible to be true, until I later confirmed, it was indeed the case.

Following that first encounter, there were nights when, whilst watching through the back kitchen window with the lights switched off, I actually saw Mr. Fox present himself on the other side of the garden gate. The animal would just stand there, at a safe distance, watching and waiting for his new found friend to join him.

When I opened the back door to let Jack out, he would immediately make for the gap in the hedge, and both dog and fox would venture off side by side, with Jack engaged in his usual sniffing of the ground, and his new companion walking a few paces behind, like some kind of night shift supervisor.

After each moonlight walk, Jack would return and the fox would make sure his friend had got home safely, before taking off again. It was all so unreal, and yet why was I so surprised, considering the many different and unusual aspects of this dog's enigmatic character?

A thousand thoughts raced through my mind. Should I photograph and record this unusual series of events for all time? I became worried that a flash from the camera might frighten the fox away. Should I notify people who were specialists in recording such incidents? There again, I would undoubtedly feel guilty at intruding upon what was so obviously a private arrangement between my dog and his unusual new acquaintance. Finally, I decided to do nothing, and just leave nature to take its course.

It wasn't every night the fox came calling;

perhaps twice or three times a week, but it was noticeable that when this small mammal with a flattened skull and pointed snout, wasn't there, Jack showed no interest in going out of doors. We virtually knew when the visitor was in attendance, when the dog would make for the back door.

Towards the end of that winter, as the nights became shorter and the new season began to take over, the fox disappeared, and was never seen to visit again. As for Jack, he continued living his life as he had always done before, pestering me to take him for runs across the fields, and often playing in the back garden with a ball or rubber ring.

As the buds on the Hawthorn hedge began to appear and the lawns grew longer, it seemed that what we had all witnessed during those cold frosty nights, hadn't really happened at all. But it had, and I will never forget having been privileged to witness such a surprising and prodigious event.

During the summer months, our grandson, Charlie, who by then was a toddler, spent a great deal of time playing in our back garden, always watched over by Jack. The dog had now found a new vacation as a baby minder, and never took his eyes off, Charlie, whether inside or outside the house.

Although there was always an adult present when our young grandson was busying himself on the back lawn, Jack would also be in attendance, often glued to the toddler's side. There was one occasion when, Charlie managed to scramble up some steps leading to the gate which divided the garden from the fields, and stood looking out through the wooden struts. As usual, Jack was on duty nearby, with his ever watchful eye on the infant.

Then a large black dog, which seemed friendly enough, approached the gate from the field side, wagging its tail and obviously hoping for some fuss. With the same speed, Jack usually reserved for chasing rats, he flew up the steps and pushed himself between, Charlie and the unwelcome visitor, barking and snarling like a wild animal infected with Rabies.

The visiting dog quickly made himself scarce, and Jack looked up at his charge, before shoving his wet nose into Charlie's little legs, which was an obvious signal for the lad to move away from the gate.

I had witnessed the whole event from the kitchen door, and once again was amazed at the human way in which the dog had responded to what he had considered to be a moment of peril.

When our grandson got a little older, we were able to take him with us for walks out on the field. Even then, Jack remained close to Charlie, watching over him like a Mother Hen.

There were occasions when our dog would disappear during daylight hours, without us noticing he was missing, albeit, not for long, and I would often scour the district in search of him. Sometimes I would find him just walking along, stopping to examine some person's garden, or standing there unobtrusively, watching a group of children at play.

There were also times, when he would be brought home by some neighbourly individual who had found him up on the village green, or standing alone outside the local Post Office, which was a favourite haunt of his, whenever he decided to stretch his legs.

In fact, whenever I visited the same establishment, I would take Jack with me and tie him to the side of the post box outside the front of the small building. Once I had concluded my business inside the Post Office, I would then return home across the fields, to allow Jack some freedom in which he could run and skip.

It was on such an occasion when, after securing the dog outside the front, I entered the Post Office and stood in a small queue, waiting to be served. Suddenly, all heads turned towards a postman who came rushing in, and anxiously enquired as to who owned the dog outside.

I instantly confessed in answer to his query,

and he immediately explained that the dog wouldn't let him gain access to the post box, which he needed to empty. Laughter echoed around the Post Office, and of course, I once again felt obliged to offer an apology to the distraught postman, before leaving the queue to go back outside and take Jack to one side, whilst the postman did his job.

Shortly after I had concluded my business there, and as we were crossing the road, intending to walk home across the fields, there was a sudden cloud burst, and the rain unexpectedly cascaded down with a vengeance. Holding Jack close to me on the lead, I ran as fast as I could into the shelter of an open sided annex, attached to the side of a nearby local hotel, where we both remained until the rain finally eased off.

Postponing my intended visit to the fields, we

began to walk home along the pavement. Near to the driveway entrance of the hotel was a broken manhole cover, and surprisingly, Jack suddenly stopped and began to growl at the partially fractured cover. At the time I didn't take much notice, and just forcibly pulled him away, before returning home.

A few days later, it was the local postman who first alerted us to yet another spectacle involving Jack, which was taking place on the opposite side of where the Post Office was located.

"Your dog's killed about a dozen rats outside the hotel," the postman explained excitedly, and referring to the same establishment where we had previously sheltered from the rain.

I quickly accompanied the postman back to where the front driveway of the hotel was situated, where I saw, Jack, standing erect, with both eyes staring down the same defective manhole he had taken an interest in previously. The dog was surrounded by trophies of at least half a dozen large sized rats, all lying dead on the ground.

I called out to him, and he turned to look at me approaching, but before coming to me, a small head popped up from the side of the manhole cover, only to be snatched rapidly by a set of teeth, shook violently, and tossed across the pavement to join its predecessors.

"That's another one," the postman confirmed, "He'll be at this until it gets dark."

"No he won't," I answered, "Not unless that hotel wants to pay for his services,"

People passing by shouted over to us, congratulating my dog on a fine performance, and jokingly hinting that he could do a job for them if needs be.

Once again, I was proud of my four legged

companion, but also admonished him for leaving the house in the first place. Following his first awareness of the presence of vermin down that particular manhole, he must have waited his first opportunity to return and do his favourite job of work. Unfortunately, it had been successfully completed without pay, but at least the hotel staff had been made to clear the pavement of Jack's furry victims, albeit there had been no infestation at the hotel itself.

Chapter Ten

Jack

When the efficacious rat catcher finally retired, his speed of movement had deserted him, as had the acuteness in his natural smell and hearing capabilities. Jack's eyesight began to fail him, cataracts being the main cause. In similar fashion to a Derby winner put out to grass, the dog now favours a much quieter and relaxed existence.

Nowadays, our long romps across the fields are not so long. Nowadays, Jack tends to remain more by my side, as we slowly make our way back down to the ancient bridge that crosses over the narrow stream in the far field, adjacent to the same quarry from which he first helped to rescue a young lamb in distress. The same quarry which was saved from greater damage by fire, thanks to his alertness. Nowadays, the arthritis in my sixteen year old terrier's front legs, restrict his movement, if only slightly, but causing sufficient discomfort to warrant a daily dose of pain killers.

Jack's heart is enlarged and pressing against his lungs, which means that medication is required to keep his breathing ability clear and fluent, and he spends more time lying on his chair, watching the world go by, with the occasional cough and splutter. Yet, he remains enthusiastic to leave the house whenever I call him.

Since being a victim of the viral infection which almost ended his life when still only in his first year, and having been monitored and treated by veterinary surgeons on a regular basis throughout most of his time with us, he has never been deterred from being in constant search of some new adventure.

His six weekly visits to see Katie, the caring vet, who is a warm and understanding young lady, whose dedicated attention keeps him mobile and virtually pain free, is now his main source of survival and a reasonable quality of life.

On occasions, I often wonder where those puppies he sired with, Mollie the Yorkshire Terrier, are now domiciled, and whether they possess the same fearless and energetic characteristics as their father.

I shall always remember those hot summer halcyon days, when we both ventured out to explore the surrounding countryside; the way in which he showed relentless bravery as he, not only faced down a wild Lynx, but chased it away, having no regard for his own safety. Some would say it was the madness of a dog without the sense to stay clear. I would call it raw courage displayed by a Jack Russell Terrier, which was highly intelligent and calculating.

How is it possible for a terrier to befriend a wild fox? And yet my dog had done so, taking early winter evening strolls with such a wild mammal, in a relationship where there was a great deal of mutual respect.

There will be no more opportunities to take television engineers off the air by biting through main cables, or to chase around a ladies hair salon, creating havoc. No, all of those indiscretions now belong to history.

There are many incidents I have shared with that small dog with a coat as white as snow, but which are too trivial to mention here, although perhaps one more comes to mind. The occasion we met a small herd of cows, which were accompanied by their calves.

At the time, Jack had run well in front of me, and without warning I found myself surrounded by beeves that looked extremely angry at my presence, so much so, they began to crowd in all around me, stamping their heavy hooves and bawling out their protests. For a brief moment I actually believed I was in some danger myself, until he came bounding back, barking and snarling, sufficiently to give those cows a change of heart, and dispersing them as quickly as they had gathered.

The number of small birds, and on one occasion even a field mouse, he found injured in some way, which resulted in each casualty being taken home with us to treat and make well. Thanks to Jack, my garage on occasions resembled an infirmary for sick wild creatures, but we never lost one and they were all eventually returned to the wild in better health than when he first found them.

I recall the only occasion I ever heard him groan, following an operation to remove his testicles, for which it took him a long time to forgive me. The veterinary surgeon who was treating him at the time suspected he might develop a tumour and advised me to have him castrated. Of course I agreed, rather than risk a more serious, life threatening situation to develop.

So, under the anesthetic he went, having taken him to the surgery one early morning. When I collected him on the following evening, we spent the whole night together, with Jack lying on my lap, faintly moaning from the pain which resulted from the operation. But, if it saved his life, it was worth the discomfort.

So, now he is an old man, one hundred and twelve years old in human terms, but no longer frolics with the lambs, or teases their mothers. Now he bides him time, moving from one chair to another, rather than leaping from one adventure into the next.

I shall always remember with pride, when Jack was still a puppy, we were invited to a dog show in Gloucestershire, where his father and a few other relatives were participating, in an effort to qualify for the annual Crufts event. His breeder, Sara was present and introduced my dog to one of the judges, who immediately advised us to show Jack at future competitions. And yet without hesitation, I politely declined. I had him for one purpose only. As a companion I needed to see him running freely about the countryside with his ears pinned back, and his eyes filled with joy. I wanted my dog to enjoy everything that would have appealed to most dogs, in particular Parson Jack Russell Terriers.

In return, my dog has given me the utmost trust and loyalty. He has taught me on occasions how to be humble and caring; he has provided me with motivation when struggling for innovation or the remedy to some difficulty. But above all, the most treasured gift he has given me, is a recognition of the need to care for other creatures, less fortunate than ourselves.

The American wildlife photographer and

television personality, Roger Caras once wrote:

Dogs have given us their absolute all. We are the centre of their universe. We are the focus of their love and faith and trust. They serve us in return for scraps. It is without a doubt the best deal man has ever made.

I for one, would agree entirely with those sentiments.

John Plimmer is the author of the popular Dan Mitchell series of books about international espionage and crime:

About the Author

John F Plimmer retired from the West Midlands force as a prominent high profile detective following a thirty one year illustrious career in which he was responsible for the investigation of more than 30 murder inquiries, all of which were detected successfully.

During a four year period working for the Regional Crime Squad and Security Forces, Plimmer participated in the introduction of professional training and support for covert agents in the West Midlands and other parts of the country. His experience in dealing with undercover operations linked him with overseas agents in Holland, Belgium, Spain, Morocco and Germany.

Following his retirement he lectured in Law at Birmingham University and became a columnist and feature writer for The Sunday Mercury and Birmingham Evening Mail. Today he frequently participates in discussions and interviews on police and legal subjects on both television and radio.

His television work has included working as a script consultant on popular programmes such as Dalziel and Pascoe and Cracker.

His published works include a number of Home Office Blue Papers on Serious Crime Management and Covert Police Handling. He is the author of a number of published books which include 'In the Footsteps of the Whitechapel Murders' (The Book Guild); Inside Track; Running with the Devil; The Whitechapel Murders and Brickbats & Tutus (House of Stratus).

He is a dedicated reader of Louis L'Amour often giving L'Amour's work as the reason for spending years researching the old pioneering west.

His western novels include 'The Invisible Gun' 'Apache Justice' and 'The Butte Conspiracy'. His popular book, 'The Cutting Edge' is a partially factual account of the biggest bank hoist ever committed in the history of the United Kingdom. The same work is the first of a series featuring Dan Mitchell, a British agent working for the Deep Cover Agency of the Foreign Office.

Other published books written by John Plimmer include:

Dan Mitchell series:

Cutting Edge
Red Mist
The Food Mountain
The Neutron Claw
Chinese Extraction
Wrangel Island
Justice Casee

Western Triology:

Tatanka Jake
Apache Justice
The Butte Conspiracy

Highwayman Series

In the Footsteps of the Highwaymen
The Wood Cutter
The Return
Four Flushers

Inside Track
Running with the Devil
In the Footsteps of Capone
The World's most Notorious Serial Killers
In the Footsteps of the Whitechapel Murders
Fallen Paragons – The story of the West Midlands
                    Serious Crime Squad
Brickbats & Tutus
Backstreet Urchins

George's War
Hilda's War
Jack the Rascal
The Victorian Detective's Case Review

Printed in Great Britain
by Amazon